The Mansa

BY

Cukuru Okeke

Table of Contents

Gifts from the Creator

- *God spoke to the Earth; it heard what was said through her ears. What resulted? A beautiful grassland. "The Earth." Allah generated life with His words.*

- *Words become flesh; you will live what you speak.*

- *We have two ears for a reason: to listen and hear our Creator. If we remain as calm as still waters, He will guide us on what to do and how to move.*

- *Listen to visualize; speak to see it.*

- *Allah spoke and said, "Let there be light," and so it came into existence.*

- *Be still, quiet, and patient. Submit your ear, and He will speak; you will hear the assignment.*

- *You have not because you ask not.*

- *Write the vision and make it plain. Read, speak, hear, and see, and it will come to pass.*

The cycle of life is often misunderstood. We are born alone, naked, with no intellect - an empty mind. Once we taste the air of life, our clock begins ticking. Like a sponge, we absorb everything we're exposed to: language, body movements, and what we hear and see. Animals, indeed, share these characteristics, taking on similar responsibilities. In the early stages of life, both humans and animals mimic what they see and speak what they hear. This aspect of the mind is profound like no other.

Endowed with a brain to comprehend what's perceived, we have two ears as impeccable receptors constantly relaying sound to the brain. Our eyes absorb light from the grassland, processing visual information. Our mouths speak life, and our nose filter our air.

In the initial stages of life, "at birth," we hear and see without being taught. Before humans grasp the concept of existence, there's no need for assistance o

4

intellect to operate these senses, which help shape the mind. Allah/God created humans in such a remarkable way; it's truly awe-inspiring. Our ears and sight operate automatically, forming our consciousness, thoughts, spoken language, and body movements.

The power of the gift of a mouth, ears, and sight from Allah/God is unparalleled. These extraordinary senses allow us to interact with the world, communicate with others, and experience the beauty of the universe. They aren't just physical attributes; they hold immense spiritual significance.

The mouth, the gateway to speech, enables us to express thoughts, feelings, and emotions. Through words, we convey love, encouragement, and compassion, uplifting those around us. This remarkable gift lets us articulate our gratitude to Allah/God, praising Him for His blessings and seeking His guidance. The power of the mouth lies not only in what we say but also in the restraint to avoid harmful words, preventing harm to others and spreading negativity.

Ears, receivers of sound, enable us to perceive the beauty of music, the melodies of nature, and the voices of our loved ones. They facilitate deep connections with others, fostering empathy and understanding. Through listening, we gain knowledge, learn from different perspectives, and build meaningful relationships. Attentive listening demonstrates respect, patience, and compassion, creating an atmosphere of harmony and unity.

Sight, the sense of vision, allows us to witness the wonders of the world, from nature's grandeur to the beauty of human connection. It opens our eyes to the signs of Allah/God's creation, reminding us of His omnipotent presence. The power of sight goes beyond our ability to see; it's about understanding the world deeply and striving for a better future.

The power of these gifted senses reminds us of our responsibility as human beings. We must use them for the benefit of ourselves and those around us. We should speak kind and wise words, listen empathetically, and use our sight for goodness and appreciation. By doing so, we honor the blessing bestowed upon us and live in alignment with our divine purpose.

The power of the gift of a mouth, ears, and sight from Allah/God is immeasurable. These senses not only allow us to perceive the physical world but also provide us with the means to connect spiritually with our Creator and fellow human beings. It is our responsibility to use these gifts thoughtfully and to employ them as tools for positive change in ourselves and in society.

In every aspect of our lives, we encounter gifts from the Creator. From the grandeur of nature to the people we cherish, there is an abundance of blessings surrounding us. These gifts remind us of our connection with a higher power and compel us to appreciate the remarkable creations that surround us.

The most precious gift of all is life itself. Each individual is a unique creation, a miracle in their own right. The complexity of the human suit and mind is a testament to the Creator's wisdom and creativity. We are gifted with the ability to think, feel, and experience the world around us.

Nature is a masterful work of art crafted by the Creator. From majestic mountains to serene oceans, every element of the natural world holds inherent beauty. The lush greenery of forests, the delicate petals of flowers, and the songs of birds are just a few examples of the gift's nature bestows upon us.

One of the Creator's greatest gifts is the ability to form meaningful connections with others. These relationships enrich our lives, bringing joy, love, and companionship. Whether it's the bond between a parent and child, the love shared between partners, or the camaraderie among friends, relationships are gifts that bring warmth and fulfillment.

Animals are an integral part of our world and a gift from the Creator. The diversity of the animal kingdom is awe-inspiring, from magnificent creatures like elephants and lions to the tiniest insects. Animals bring us companionship, teach us important lessons and remind us of the Creator's nurturing spirit.

Emotions are a gift that allows us to experience life deeply. Joy, love, sorrow, and awe are just a few of the myriad emotions that enrich our existence. The bring color and meaning to our lives, allowing us to connect with others and understand ourselves on a deeper level.

The ability to create is an innate gift that mirrors the Creator's own creativity. Whether through art, music, writing, or any other form of expression, creativity connects us to something greater than ourselves. It allows us to bring to life the ideas and visions that reside within us, uniting us with the divine spark of inspiration.

Knowledge is a gift that expands our horizons and empowers us to understand the world and our place within it. The pursuit of knowledge is a lifelong journey, and each new piece of information we learn is a gift from the Creator, opening our minds and broadening our understanding.

Forgiveness is a gift that liberates both the giver and the receiver. It releases us from the burden of resentment and allows for healing and growth. Forgiveness is an act of compassion and understanding, reflecting the Creator's capacity for unconditional love and acceptance.

Hear the Voice

- *The Creator spoke words and gave assignments to the Earth.*

- *Allah/God also speaks to us, providing insight and assignments on this grassland.*

- *The Earth is quiet and still when she hears Allah/God. As humans, we are made in His image, so shouldn't we hear Him as clearly as Mother Nature does? Cease from loud confusion and attune your ears to "hear the voice."*

- *Connect with Allah/God and be submissive welcoming His voice. Listen through both ears to understand what is given. Visualize the task and act accordingly.*

- *Being individually gifted to exist on Earth through Allah/God is one of the many blessings. Seize the opportunity to seek His present voice. Understanding your assignment will lead to a purpose-driven*

10

lifestyle. Clear your mind of confusion and distractions that divert you from Allah/God. We all face worldly challenges, but we have choices.

Let's embark on a captivating exploration into the mystical realm of hearing the voice of Allah/God. Here, we aim to provide guidance and insights to those seeking a deeper connection with the divine. Embark on an enlightening journey as we delve into the realms of spiritual awakening and discover the whispers of Allah/God.

We unveil the significance of the seeking soul - an individual's deep yearning to hear the voice of Allah/God. We discuss the importance of an open heart, sincere intentions, and a willingness to embark on a spiritual quest. Understanding the true essence of seeking is the foundation for unraveling the divine connection.

Prayer and reflection are the keys to opening the gates of communication with Allah/God. We delve into the significance of establishing a strong connection with daily prayer and how it acts as a conduit for hearing the voice of Allah/God. Reflection, contemplation, and gratitude are vital components in nurturing our spirituality and attuning our hearts to the divine.

Silence is a powerful tool to attune our inner selves to the voice of Allah/God. By quieting our minds and creating a sacred space for introspection, we awaken our souls to the divine whispers that are often obscured by the noise of the world.

A pure heart becomes a receptive vessel for the divine voice. It's importance of purify our intentions, seek forgiveness, and engage in acts of kindness. By focusing on spirituality and self-improvement, we cleanse our hearts and remove any barriers that hinder our ability to hear the voice of Allah/God.

We discover the subtle signs and messages that Allah/God sends our way. Whether through nature dreams, or synchronicities, divine signs can offer profound guidance and reassurance. By learning to recognize and interpret these signs, our connection with Allah/God grows stronger, and His voice becomes more audible.

The Gift of Revelation

Delving into the beauty of divine revelation, we explore the importance of studying the Quran and the teachings of the Prophet Muhammad (peace be upon him). Our understanding of these sacred texts allows us to gain deeper insights into the divine plan and opens doors to hearing the voice of Allah directly through His revealed words.

Embracing Patience and Trust

Patience and trust are essential virtues on our spiritual journey. Trusting in Allah/God's wisdom and divine timing enables us to surrender to His will and opens doors to hearing His voice in the most unexpected ways.

The voice of Allah/God is not reserved for a select few; it is accessible to all who seek it with a sincere heart. By following the guidance offered in this book and embarking on a personal exploration, you will discover the divine whispers that will enlighten and transform your life. May this journey lead you to a deeper connection with the divine, as you hear the voice of Allah/God echoing within your being.

Drugs and alcohol, when abused, can have detrimental effects on an individual's mental state and hinder their spiritual connection with Allah. Substance abuse can lead to severe psychological disorders, such as anxiety, depression, and psychosis. These conditions can cloud a person's judgment, impair their cognitive functioning, and disrupt their ability to think clearly and make rational decisions.

Furthermore, drugs and alcohol can interfere with an individual's ability to concentrate and focus on their spirituality. They can create a false sense of euphoria or relaxation, which can distract a person from seeking a deep spiritual connection with Allah. These substances can also cause feelings of guilt and shame, further separating individuals from their relationship with their faith.

Moreover, substance abuse can contribute to a cycle of dependence and addiction, where individuals may prioritize obtaining and using drugs or alcohol over fulfilling their spiritual obligations. This can lead to neglect of religious practices, strained relationships with family and loved ones, and a loss of self-control and self-discipline that is essential for a strong connection with Allah/God.

To maintain a healthy mental state and a strong bond with Allah/God, it is crucial to stay away from drugs and alcohol and seek alternative, healthy coping mechanisms. Engaging in regular prayer, surrounding oneself with a supportive community, and seeking professional help for substance abuse can be essential steps towards recovery and strengthening one's spiritual connection.

The consumption of toxic substances in earthly vessels will deteriorate the mental state, damaging the physical state. Humans often succumb to an array of toxins, and their physical cravings can distance them from Allah/God.

Examples include toxic giggle water, strong drink, and alcohol. Toxic giggle water negatively impacts the mental state and, subsequently, the physical state, leading to complications within your earthly vessel and resulting in early demise.

Examples of other toxic substances are delusion dust, blue magic, and drugs. These substances poison the mind, elevating consciousness to higher planes, but often resulting in blurred judgment.

Examples like smoke, hash, and cigarettes introduce harsh, polluted airborne particles into our lungs, leading to internal cancers and complications.

Some individuals inject impurities into their bloodstream in pursuit of a heightened sensation, resulting in severe health risks such as heart infections, collapsed veins, overdoses, and the potential transmission of diseases like hepatitis B, hepatitis C, and AIDS.

Toxic acts damage not only our physical and mental well-being but also our connection to Allah/God. They cloud the passageway to our Creator, hindering our assignments on this grassland. What are we here for? These habits are distractions that create distance between you and the divine.

Indulging in these toxic acts may lead Allah/God to consume you with habits that create a routine, which ultimately leads to "your death."

We destroy ourselves due to a lack of knowledge. Daily on this grassland, humans destroy their earthly suits through ignorance, violence, and negative thoughts towards themselves and others. Anger and hatred vibrate at lower frequencies, bringing us mentally to our lower selves. Strife, injury, and death are the consequences when operating within this frequency.

Maintain a calm demeanor, pausing your thoughts, words, and actions when within this magnetic field of ignorance. Inhale fresh air while exhaling the hazardous fog. Breathing through dark points cleanses your brain channels of violent thoughts.

Yesterday is gone, and tomorrow is in the womb. One of life's beauties is the opportunity to create better days.

Earthly Suit

- *Health is a crucial factor in this grassland. In the early days, humans primarily dined on leaves, fruits from trees, shrubs, and herbs.*

- *We consumed what grew from this grassland, rather than what walked upon it.*

- *Trees and humans share similar characteristics. Both are composed of water and breathe air, albeit in distinct ways. Humans inhale oxygen and exhale carbon dioxide, while trees absorb carbon dioxide and release oxygen. Trees and humans are mutually dependent.*

- *Why can a tree outlive a human by 5 to 3 lifetimes, even though our structures are similar?*

- *Health is wealth, wealth isn't health.*

In the early days of human existence, our primary source of sustenance was the natural bounty of the grasslands. We feasted on leaves, fruits from trees, shrubs, and herbs. Instead of consuming what roamed the land, we opted to partake in what grew from it. This dietary choice was a harmonious alignment with the environment and our needs.

It's intriguing to note that humans and trees share strikingly similar characteristics. Both are primarily composed of water and engage with the atmosphere, albeit in distinct ways. Humans breathe in oxygen and exhale carbon dioxide, while trees absorb carbon dioxide and release oxygen. This intricate web of life underscores our mutual dependence on the natural world.

One might ponder: Why can a tree outlive a human by 5 to 9 lifetimes, even though our structural composition bears resemblances? The answer lies in the intricate relationship between lifestyle, health, and longevity. Health is indeed wealth, but wealth is not health.

Our modern-day diets, often inundated with processed and man-made products, have inadvertently introduced contaminants into our earthly suits. The consumption of animal products, plagued by toxins and pathogens, unknowingly creates an ideal habitat for disease, parasites, and worms. The thought of feasting on a human-like corpse is far from normal or healthy. Our suits are designed to thrive on earthly grass vegetation and fruits, which serve as both a healing mechanism and an energy catalyst.

Years of adherence to a carnivorous lifestyle have altered our hunger signals, compelling us to gravitate towards flesh over fresh, nutrient-rich vegetables and hydration from water. This prolonged indulgence in animal flesh has been linked to various health issues from cancer and diabetes to high blood pressure. But how can we break free from these ingrained patterns?

Fasting, particularly water and fruit fasting for 30, 60, or 90 days, can serve as a potent method to break these cravings and eliminate parasites. This approach not only rejuvenates the body but also cleanses it of the accumulated effects of a carnivorous diet. The path to healing and longevity lies in reconnecting with the essence of nature's offerings.

The tree of life symbolizes this rejuvenation. To ensure a lengthy existence on this grassland, we must prioritize the preservation and well-being of our earthly suits. We need to respect our suits, cherish them, and understand that no task or assignment can be fulfilled effectively with a polluted vessel. The choice to honor our health and embrace a more natural, plant-based diet is not just a personal one but an act of stewardship towards the planet and a testament to our interconnectedness with nature.

Souls

A soul on this grassland is one of the greatest creations in our existence. One of Allah/God's most astonishing works is a soul. Whether it's a human suit or an animal form, a soul must be attached to flesh to operate in this world. If it's a human soul, it will only operate within a human suit, and an animal soul within an animal suit.

We've all heard the saying, "I've been here before."

The soul can only return to its original 1st dimensional form, whether human or animal. Human souls inhabit human suits, while animal souls inhabit animal suits.

For example, consider the story of Noah's Ark, which most of us remember. Allah/God appointed him a mission. Within those instructions, Noah was to build a boat, gather his family and friends (both male and female), and animals of different sexes. Why? Well, it's common sense! Humans reproduce within human suits, and animals reproduce within their own forms, allowing souls to attach and repopulate life. So, Allah/God cleansed the Earth of evil, wiping out various human and animal suits, but the souls remained. The grassland is now purified and let us now reprogram the souls within earthly suits.

The 1st dimension is life born of flesh and blood on this grassland, operating within human or animal suits.

The 2nd dimension is consciousness, the knowledge of who and what you are while experiencing life on this grassland.

The 3rd dimension is death, where your soul departs your earthly suit, returning your flesh to the ground.

All human and animal suits return to the Earths stomach, but the soul remains aware, entering the 3rd dimension.

During an autopsy, regardless of the cause of death, such as a gunshot wound to the head, when the earthly suit is examined by a forensic pathologist, only flesh, bone, and blood is visible to the naked eye. The brain's primary function is to control the suit, limbs, and internal processes. Where do you think the soul resides? Some may say the heart, and many believe it is in the pineal gland, typically within the brain.

What I am trying to emphasize is this: Our soul is not mechanical or computerized; it is a creation invisible to the eye, beyond the scope of measurement or construction by scientists. My theory is that the soul is a conscious state that exists within controlling earthly suits, whether human or animal. Allah/God created the soul to experience the beauty and wonders of life on this grassland, but fleshly suits cannot connect with higher powers, only a soul can. Thus, we were not designed merely to exist without hearing and communicating with the creator. Meditation, prayer, and a spiritual connection with Allah/God while in our earthly bodies must be achieved by all humans to gain the full experience. Discipline your flesh, refrain from toxic deeds, and cultivate a clear and clean consciousness to access secure connection with Allah/God.

The soul remains tethered to the earthly suit until separation by death, or it dwells safely in the 3rd dimension while presently on this grassland.

Dimensions

All flesh returns to the earth's stomach, but your soul remains awake, entering the 3rd dimension.

Ladies and gentlemen, I am here to share an extraordinary experience. I entered the 3rd dimension with my soul and consciousness while hovering over my earthly suit. I heard from Allah/God, and He showed me my previous earthly suit, "Mansa Musa."

Experiencing the 3rd dimension, detaching from my earthly suit, and connecting with Allah/God was profoundly chilling. To hear our creator at a higher frequency, I had to separate from my fleshly vessel, my earthly suit. Most, if not all, will never experience this due to mental disconnection. I was able to drift into this realm with my soul lingering over my earthly suit, which allowed me to hear Allah/God. He permitted me to control my body like a puppet, which felt incredibly strange.

During this journey, I conversed with Allah/God while observing this world from a different perspective. My heart raced due to the chilling experience, and I heard Him through my soul, stating that He controls everything, that exists inside and outside me.

"Mansa Musa, ruler and king of Mali in Western Africa."

My first out-of-body experience occurred in 2009 at the age of 19. This detachment from my earthly suit was surreal; I thought I had lost my mind. As I drifted out of my shell, it felt as if demons had enveloped me. Looking down at my suit I could see shadowed spirits crawling over my flesh, and evil screeching in my ears from the wrongdoings of this world. I calmed myself and began to pray during this mind-boggling event. Slowly returning to my body, I kept chanting my prayer. In that isolated moment, everything returned to normal, and I was reattached, drenched in sweat. As I gazed at myself in the mirror, my eyes were bloodshot red, and I knew I had witnessed the power of Allah/God and the strength o

my words.

The power of prayer: Our tongue is the mos

powerful weapon on this grassland; what you speak

will manifest.

My second out-of-body experience occurred in

2020 at the age of 30. During this separation from my

suit, I wondered what was happening. It was a similar

experience to 2009, but without the presence o

demons. Instead, Allah/God detached me to witness

the sins and evils within other human bodies. We all

carry some form of spirit, or many spirits, based on

our life choices—good or evil. Struggling to return to

my body, Allah/God controlled my every move in

this life's video game. He did not allow me to pray as

I did during my first experience; instead, He granted

me an Arabic language. While praying in Arabic

Allah/God positioned my body in the Islamic stance

with tears in my eyes. It was a profound experience

that revealed my past soul was Islamic.

My third out-of-body experience occurred in 2023. In this phase, Allah revealed my true identity and the origin of my soul. Subconsciously familiar with previous events, this did not shock me. This time, Allah/God directed me to the internet. I typed in two unfamiliar words, "Mansa Musa." While researching this name, Allah/God changed my interpretation, and I found myself reading from right to left in Arabic. I was not even aware of the change until my consciousness shifted. Still outside my suit, I began to have flashbacks of ruling as a king. In this vision, I sat at the foot of a grand feast table, surrounded by gold, wearing king-like attire. In Allah/God's presence, He reminded me of His creations, including the world and everything in it. Our ears, mouth, and sight are His most powerful gifts to us, and everything He created has a soul. Animals will always be animals, and humans will always be humans, with no souls crossing over into different suits.

This reminded me of the story of Moses, which I reference in the chapter on souls. Moses was assigned to bring one pair of human males and females, along

with pairs of different-sex animals, aboard his ark
Through this act, and the history of preproduction
earthly bodies, souls are born into human and anima
forms.

Allah/God created this world for earthly suits to
experience joy, happiness, and laughter. Despite the
creeping evils, He has made beautiful thing
common. This world is unique, as are humans who
breathe air, while ocean and sea creatures inhale
water. Uncommon acts surround us.

As humans on this earth, we must connect with
Allah/God, listen to His voice, and be sensitive to it
Let's hear through both ears, speak what He tells us
and visualize the extraordinary acts He appoints. Find
your calling, your appointed role, your gift on this
grassland through Allah/God, and know who you are.

Disconnect, Connect

We grapple with the choice of exercising our free will to either advance or hinder ourselves. In a world shrouded by ignorance, foolishness, and dark imaginations, the path to righteousness may appear obscured. However, one of the many blessings bestowed upon us by Allah/God is diverse minds that can guide our earthly suits through this complex terrain. It is imperative that we refrain from tainting our earthly suits with wrongdoing or negativity, as they can give birth to violence, hatred, strife, anger, and madness. Instead, let us nurture thoughts of happiness, laughter, peace, and love to manifest better earthly suits.

Thinking oneself into good health, greatness, a royal priesthood, wealth, and abundance is not a mere aspiration; it is a realization of the life Allah/God intends for us on this grassland. The journey to self-mastery begins with strengthening our connection with Allah/God, one step at a time, mastering ourselves before imparting this wisdom to others. The challenges of self-mastery, once conquered, unlock greatness in every aspect of life.

As we engage with the diverse earthly suits around us, it is crucial to carefully observe those whom we invite into our private dwellings, our sanctuaries. We must not be deceived by kind gestures and smiles, for behind laughter and good times, darker intentions may lurk. Wisely assess the individuals you choose to associate with and remain vigilant in the places you frequent. A sound mind coupled with wisdom can withstand deception, allowing us to learn from those we encounter and gain insights into their true characters, whether genuine or malevolent.

Life on this grassland is a valuable experience, and as the saying goes, "no pain, no gain." Heavy hearts, weary spirits, and broken souls are but temporary states; harsh, icy winters do not endure.

The wealthy and renowned may attract many friends, but the authenticity of these associations can be challenging to discern. Conversely, the poor and lesser-known may have fewer friendships, making it easier to recognize the true character of those they encounter. In the search for genuine friendships, humility is measured during the lowest and most challenging times, not during moments of prosperity.

In this realm of life, we are bound by the law of nature, reaping what we sow. We are magnetic entities, attracting and repelling based on our actions:

- Sow love to reap love.

- Sow peace to harvest peace.

- Generosity begets generosity.

- A smile given will return in kind.

- Evil sown will seek you out.

- Hatred planted will breed hatred.

- Life blossoms from well-nurtured seeds.

- Your actions determine the energy you attract, as you reap what you sow in this environment.

Engaging in trade, whether involving money, raw materials, or valuable goods, can either foster positive or negative tension. Ethical business practices build credibility, loyalty, and longevity, while unethical transactions fuel conflict, deceit, and risk. Always question sources, verify references, test everything and trust no one to avoid calamity.

Never limit your potential; diligently seek knowledge to bolster your qualifications. Your current position in life hinges on what you know. If you don't seek, you won't find. Acquiring knowledge early in life lays the foundation for a fulfilling existence in later years.

Ultimately, the only person impeding your progress is the one you share your toothbrush with. Human bodies do not prosper on this grassland due to a lack of key components such as faith, consistency, routine, and focus. Allow the rivers of your mind to flow freely, unburdened by life's dilemmas and mental boundaries.

Man & Woman

Society has categorized the sexes into various roles. Men often bear pejorative labels, while women are burdened with derogatory slurs. The question arises: Why are masculinity and feminism under threat when men require the nurturing womb and women the seeds of life? In today's world, both men and women often lack a profound understanding of their gender's intrinsic meaning. The ideal roles become obscured by a fabricated societal image, leading to identity confusion.

Upbringing plays a pivotal role in shaping individuals. We've all heard the adage, "the apple doesn't fall far from the tree," and it holds true in many cases. We inherit traits from our parents, role models, and the environments in which we are raised. Consequently, we unconsciously mimic the roles and positions we observe in these people and places.

For instance, how can a boy comprehend the role of a man or the responsibilities of a father when such a figure is absent from his life? Similarly, how can a man truly understand how to love a woman if he never had a mother figure present? In these cases the mental aspects of their gender roles remain unfulfilled, and individuals often resort to self teaching to grasp these roles internally.

Likewise, a woman may find it challenging to understand and operate with men if she never had father figure at home. Her internal self-education becomes essential to grasp the dynamics of womanhood and her role within it.

Man and woman were created in the image of higher power, designed to exist in perfect harmony. Yet, today, we witness a misalignment. This misalignment arises from the swapping of gender roles, the denigration of both sexes, the fierce competition between them, and the controversies surrounding their existence.

Society encourages us to guard ourselves from the opposite sex due to past experiences of upbringing, heartbreak, and betrayal. This emotional armor leads us to hold onto past traumas, hindering our freedom and future happiness.

Tensions and conflicts between men and women have been present throughout history. While there is undoubtedly animosity between the sexes, it is crucial to delve into the root causes of this division and promote love and unity for harmonious coexistence. This discussion will examine the reasons for the existence of this animosity, the societal factors contributing to it, and advocate for love and understanding as the bridge between the sexes.

Throughout history, societal norms and expectations have perpetuated stereotypes, biases, and discrimination, creating unequal power dynamics, resource distribution, and opportunities. This has sown the seeds of resentment, which can evolve into hatred and animosity between the sexes.

In many societies, women have endured historical oppression, inequality, and discrimination. This systematic oppression has bred deep-seated anger, justly directed at those who have benefited from the patriarchal system - men. Conversely, men have faced

societal pressures to conform to narrow definitions o
masculinity, resulting in emotional repression and the
reinforcement of harmful narratives about women
further contributing to underlying animosity.

Differences in communication styles between mer
and women have also played a significant role in
perpetuating the divide. Men tend to be more direc
and task-oriented, while women lean towards buildin,
connections and expressing emotions, leading to
misunderstandings and frustrations.

To break the cycle of hatred and division, fosterin,
empathy and understanding between men an
women is essential. Both genders must recognize tha
their conflicts and disparities are rooted in societa
structures rather than inherent differences. Rathe
than blaming one another, individuals must strive t
be allies, challenge gender stereotypes, and suppo
each other in dismantling oppressive systems.

In conclusion, the animosity between men an
women is an unfortunate product of historical, socia
and cultural factors. It is imperative that both sexe
recognize the importance of love, empathy, an

understanding. Our collective goal should be to dismantle systems and societal norms perpetuating division, replacing them with an environment of respect, equality, and unity. In doing so, we can create a world where men and women celebrate and support each other, fostering a harmonious and egalitarian society.

Opposites attract – male and female.

Why don't we cherish each other and the unique qualities that the opposite sex brings? Women, do you not appreciate the strength and stability that masculinity offers? Men, do you not yearn for the warmth and tenderness of femininity?

While we share common features, our programming, DNA, and essence are fundamentally distinct. No two individuals, whether man, woman, or any living being, are alike.

Before making a commitment to marriage, it's crucial to evaluate your potential partner. Ladies, take your time with the significant "yes, I do." Don't be swayed by childhood fairytales or public perceptions. Can that knight in shining armor provide you with love, protection, and emotional security? Is he financially stable? Can he lead and guide your life? Do you trust this man to make decisions that will shape your future? Can he be your rock?

For those considering proposing to a woman, ask yourself: Is she gentle, calm, and a good listener? Is she supportive and capable of managing finances responsibly? Does she bring peace, comfort, and care to your life?

Combative relationships, disagreements, pride, dishonesty, lack of communication, infidelity, and betrayal are not the foundations of enduring unions. A lifelong partnership should be meticulously chosen with wisdom and care.

In conclusion, the animosity between the sexes can be mitigated by understanding, empathy, and a shared commitment to building relationships based on love, respect, and equality. Celebrating our differences and fostering harmonious partnerships can lead to a more unified and egalitarian society.

Bloodline

A bloodline refers to the lineage or ancestral line of a person, tracing their family origins and genetic heritage through generations. This concept is deeply rooted in numerous cultures and carries great significance. It not only defines an individual's identity but also exerts an influence on their social, cultural and genetic aspects of life.

By acknowledging and embracing one's bloodline individuals can pay homage to the accomplishments values, and challenges of their forebears. This sense of connection can inspire a heightened sense of purpose, motivating individuals to contribute to the betterment of their family, community, and society at large.

The bloodline plays a pivotal role in shaping individual identities, linking them to their cultural roots, preserving their genetic heritage, and providing a sense of continuity. This concept encompasses both positive and challenging dimensions, influencing social status, cultural identity, and even health. Understanding and appreciating one's bloodline can help foster a stronger sense of identity and a profound appreciation for one's ancestors, ultimately guiding individuals toward leaving a legacy cherished by future generations.

Cukuru Okeke was born to a Black American mother and a father of half Nigerian descent, with his mother being of Black American heritage and his father of full Nigerian background. Growing up with exposure to two different belief systems broadened his religious perspective. While he acknowledges similarities between Christianity and Islamic studies, his perception of Allah/God aligns more closely with Islamic beliefs when considering facts and history.

As we progress intellectually, some of us study and rely on our own understanding, while others adhere to what they know. Our diverse ethnic backgrounds often lead us to follow specific belief systems, with some individuals having a deep understanding of their roots, while others accept what's been passed down through generational traditions. In the case of

Cukuru, his bloodline traces back to Mali in Western Africa, and he identifies as Islamic. This knowledge was acquired through his personal connections and experiences, rather than through the family that raised him.

Cukuru highlights the enduring nature of the soul explaining that, once separated from our earthly existence, the soul seeks a new journey guided by Allah/God. He encourages self-discovery regarding one's origin and purpose, emphasizing the importance of understanding who you are, where you come from, and what your role is in this world. To achieve this, he suggests blocking out external distractions like media, materialism, and fabricated desires that cloud our understanding. By seeking connection with Allah/God and embracing purpose-driven life, one can attain clarity and enlightenment.

In conclusion, knowing one's bloodline appreciating one's heritage, and seeking a spiritual connection can lead to a more profound understanding of one's purpose and identity enriching both individual lives and the legacy left for future generations.

Know who you are!

Made in the USA
Monee, IL
29 January 2024

51913275R00026